Prologue: 1815, Digne

Jean Valjean, released on parole after 19 years on the chain gang, finds that the yellow ticket-of-leave he must, by law, display condemns him to be an outcast. Only the saintly Bishop of Digne treats him kindly and Valjean, embittered by years of hardship, repays him by stealing some silver.

Valjean is caught and brought back by police, and is astonished when the Bishop lies to the police to save him, also giving him two precious candlesticks. Valjean decides to start his life anew.

1823, Montreuil-sur-Mer

Eight years have passed and Valjean, having broken his parole and changed his name to Monsieur Madeleine, has risen to become both a factory owner and Mayor. (No.1, 'At the End of the Day'). One of his workers, Fantine, has a secret illegitimate child. When the other women discover this, they demand her dismissal. The foreman, whose advances she has rejected, throws her out. (No.2, 'I Dreamed a Dream').

Desperate for money to pay for medicines for her daughter, Fantine sells her locket, her hair, and then joins the whores in selling herself. Utterly degraded by her new trade, she gets into a fight with a prospective customer and is about to be taken to prison by Javert when 'The Mayor' arrives and demands she be taken to hospital instead.

The Mayor then rescues a man pinned down by a runaway cart. Javert is reminded of the abnormal strength of convict 24601 Jean Valjean, a parole-breaker whom he has been tracking for years but who, he says, has just been recaptured. Valjean, unable to see an innocent man go to prison in his place, confesses to the court that he is prisoner 24601.

At the hospital, Valjean promises the dying Fantine to find and look after her daughter Cosette. Javert arrives to arrest him, but Valjean escapes.

1823, Montfermeil

Cosette has been lodged for five years with the Thénadiers who run an inn, horribly abusing the little girl whom they use as a skivvy while indulging their own daughter, Eponine (Nos. 3 & 4, 'Castle on a Cloud' & 'Master of the House'). Valjean finds Cosette fetching water in the dark. He pays the Thénadiers to let him take Cosette away and takes her to Paris. But Javert is still on his tail . . . (No. 5, 'Stars').

1832, Paris

Nine years later, there is great unrest in the city because of the likely demise of the popular leader General Lamarque, the only man left in the Government who shows any feeling for the poor. The urchin Gavroche is in his element mixing with the whores and beggars of the capital. Among the street-gangs is one led by Thénadier and his wife, which sets upon Jean Valjean and Cosette.

They are rescued by Javert, who does not recognise Valjean until after he has made good his escape. The Thénadiers' daughter Eponine, who is secretly in love with student Marius, reluctantly agrees to help him find Cosette, with whom he has fallen in love.

At a political meeting in a small café, a group of idealistic students prepares for the revolution they are sure will erupt on the death of General Lamarque. When Gavroche brings the news of the General's death, the students, led by Enjolras, stream out into the streets to whip up popular support. (No.6, 'Do You Hear the People Sing?'). Only Marius is distracted, by thoughts of the mysterious Cosette.

Cosette is consumed by thoughts of Marius, with whom she has fallen in love (Nos.7&8, 'In My Life' and 'A Heart Full of Love'). Valjean realises that his 'daughter' is changing very quickly but refuses to tell her anything of her past. In spite of her own feelings for Marius, Eponine sadly brings him to Cosette and then prevents an attempt by her father's gang to rob Valjean's house. Valjean, convinced it was Javert who was lurking outside his house, tells Cosette they must prepare to flee the country.

On the eve of the revolution, the students and Javert see the situation from their different viewpoints; Cosette and Marius part in despair of ever meeting again; Eponine mourns the loss of Marius; and Valjean looks forward to the security of exile. The Thénadiers, meanwhile, dream of rich pickings underground from the chaos to come.

The students prepare to build the barricade. Marius, noticing that Eponine has joined the insurrection, sends her with a letter to Cosette, which is intercepted at the Rue Plumet by Valjean. Eponine decides, despite what he has said to her, to rejoin Marius at the Barricade. (No.9, 'On My Own').

The barricade is built and the revolutionaries defy an army warning that they must give up or die. Gavroche exposes Javert as a police spy. In trying to return to the barricade, Eponine is shot and killed. (No.10, 'A Little Fall of Rain'). Valjean arrives at the barricades in search of Marius. He is given the chance to kill Javert but instead lets him go.

The students settle down for a night on the barricade (No.11, 'Drink with Me') and in the quiet of the night, Valjean prays to God to save Marius from the onslaught which is to come (No.12 'Bring Him Home'). The next day, with ammunition running low, Gavroche runs out to collect more and is shot. The rebels are all killed, including their leader Enjolras.

Valjean escapes into the sewers with the unconscious Marius. After meeting Thénadier, who is robbing the corpses of the rebels, he emerges into the light only to meet Javert once more. He pleads for time to deliver the young man to hospital. Javert decides to let him go and, his unbending principles of justice shattered by Valjean's own mercy, he kills himself by throwing himself into the swollen River Seine.

A few months later, Marius, unaware of the identity of his rescuer, has recovered and recalls, at Cosette's side, the days of the barricade where all his friends have lost their lives. (No.13, 'Empty Chairs at Empty Tables'). Valjean confesses the truth of his past to Marius and insists that after the young couple are married, he must go away rather than taint the sanctity and safety of their union.

At Marius and Cosette's wedding, the Thénadiers try to blackmail Marius. Thénadier says Cosette's 'father' is a murderer and as proof produces a ring which he stole from the corpse in the sewers the night the barricades fell. It is Marius' own ring and he realises it was Valjean who rescued him that night. He and Cosette go to Valjean where Cosette learns for the first time of her own history before the old man dies, joining the spirits of Fantine, Eponine and all those who died on the barricades.

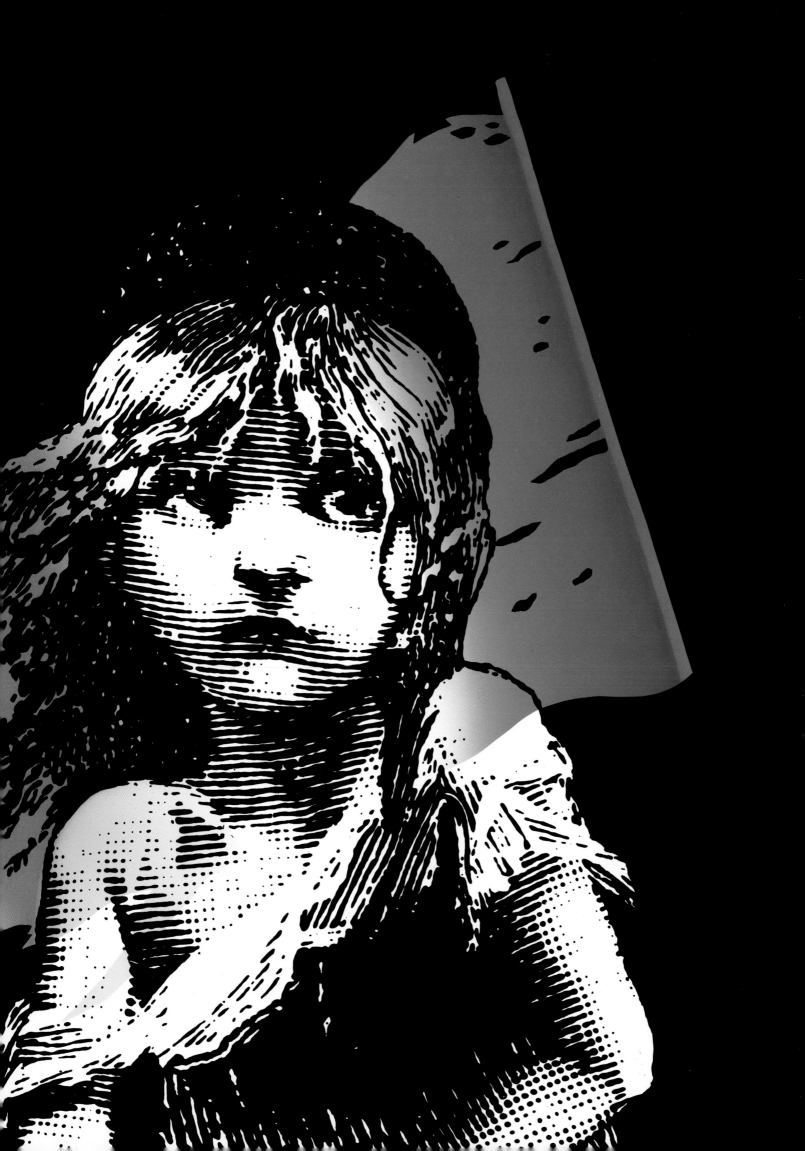

At the End of the Day

Music by CLAUDE-MICHEL SCHÖNBERG
Lyrics by HERBERT KRETZMER
Original Text by ALAIN BOUBLIL and JEAN-MARC NATEL

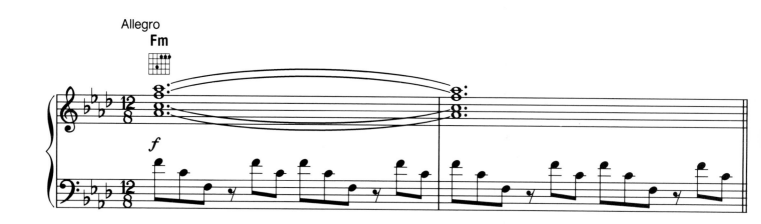

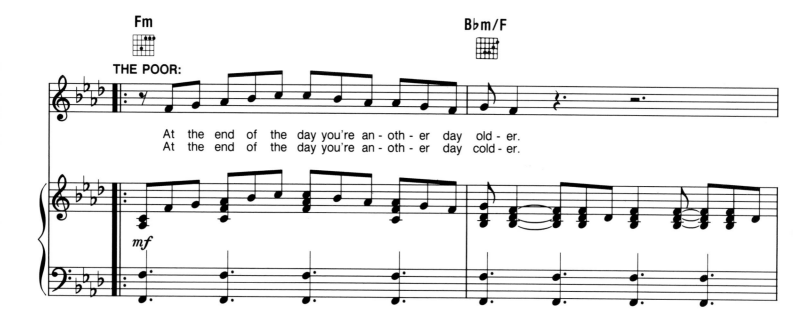

THE POOR:

At the end of the day you're an-oth-er day old-er.
At the end of the day you're an-oth-er day cold-er.

And that's all you can say for the life of the poor.
And the shirt on your back does-n't keep out the chill.

It's a
And the

I Dreamed a Dream

Music by CLAUDE-MICHEL SCHÖNBERG
Lyrics by HERBERT KRETZMER
Original Text by ALAIN BOUBLIL and JEAN-MARC NATEL

Who Am I?

Music by CLAUDE-MICHEL SCHÖNBERG
Lyrics by HERBERT KRETZMER
Original Text by ALAIN BOUBLIL and JEAN-MARC NATEL

VALJEAN: Who am I? Can I con-demn this man to slav-er-y, pre-tend I do not see his ag - o - ny? This in-no-cent who wears my face who goes to judge-ment in my place. Who am I?__ Can I con-ceal my-self for-ev-er more, pre-tend I'm not the man I

Castle on a Cloud

Music by CLAUDE-MICHEL SCHÖNBERG
Lyrics by HERBERT KRETZMER
Original Text by ALAIN BOUBLIL and JEAN-MARC NATEL

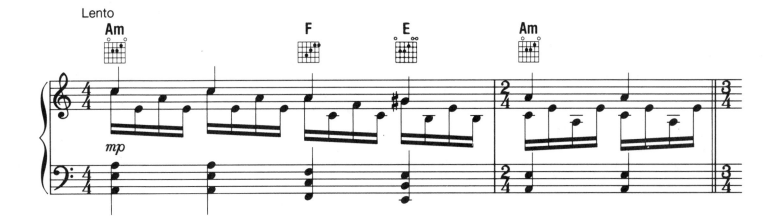

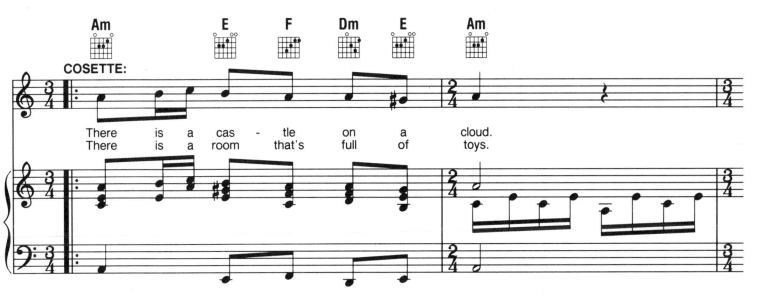

There is a cas - tle on a cloud.
There is a room that's full of toys.

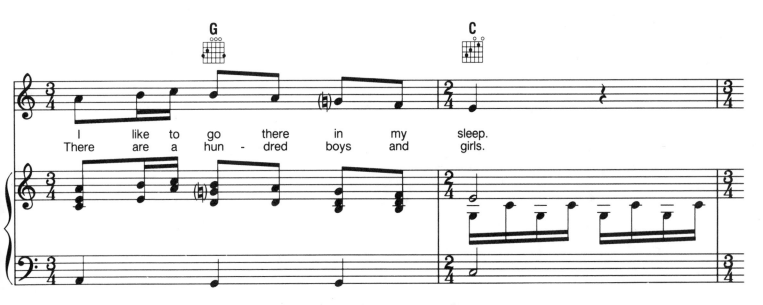

I like to go there in my sleep.
There are a hun - dred boys and girls.

Master of the House

Music by CLAUDE-MICHEL SCHÖNBERG
Lyrics by HERBERT KRETZMER
Original Text by ALAIN BOUBLIL and JEAN-MARC NATEL

Stars

Music by CLAUDE-MICHEL SCHÖNBERG
Lyrics by HERBERT KRETZMER and ALAIN BOUBLIL

Do You Hear the People Sing?

Music by CLAUDE-MICHEL SCHÖNBERG
Lyrics by HERBERT KRETZMER
Original Text by ALAIN BOUBLIL and JEAN-MARC NATEL

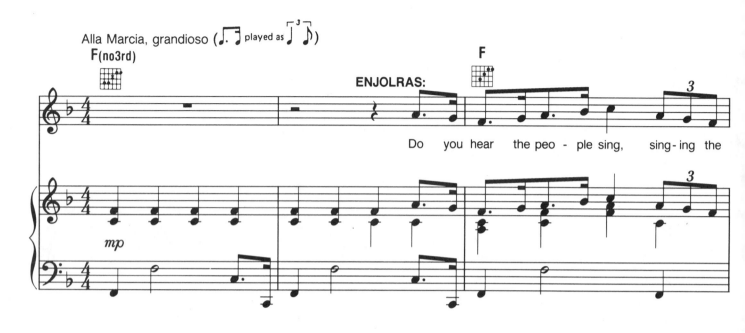

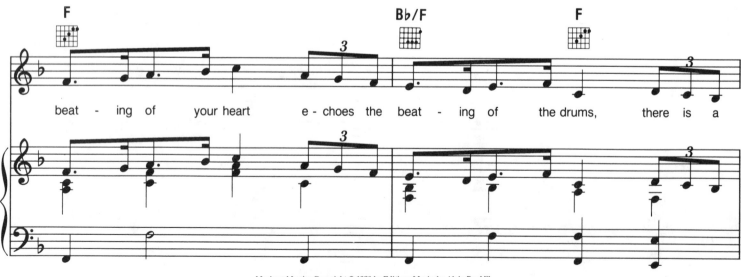

44

In My Life

Music by CLAUDE-MICHEL SCHÖNBERG
Lyrics by HERBERT KRETZMER
Original Text by ALAIN BOUBLIL and JEAN-MARC NATEL

learn. Truth is giv-en by God to us all in our time, in our

turn.

MARIUS:

In my

life she has burst like the mu-sic of an-gels, the light of the sun. And my

A Heart Full of Love

Music by CLAUDE-MICHEL SCHÖNBERG
Lyrics by HERBERT KRETZMER
Original Text by ALAIN BOUBLIL and JEAN-MARC NATEL

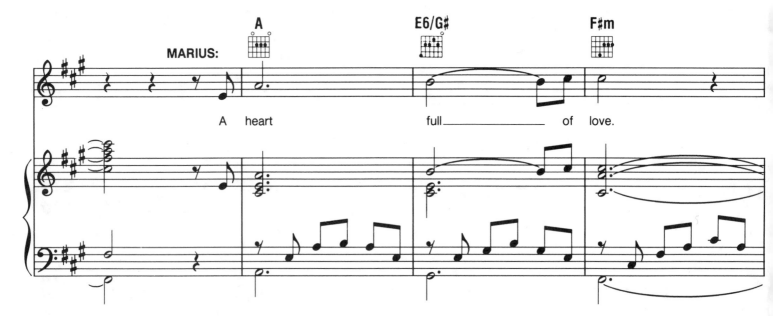

MARIUS:

A heart full_____ of love.

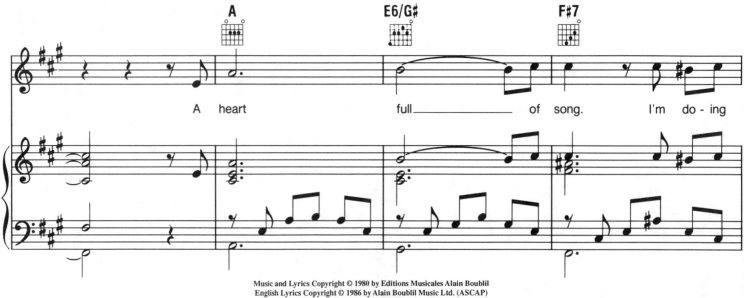

A heart full_____ of song. I'm do-ing

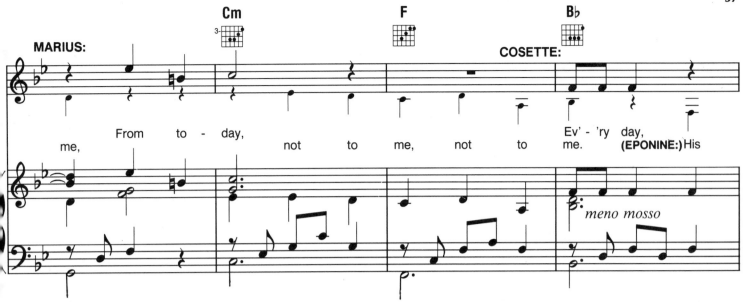

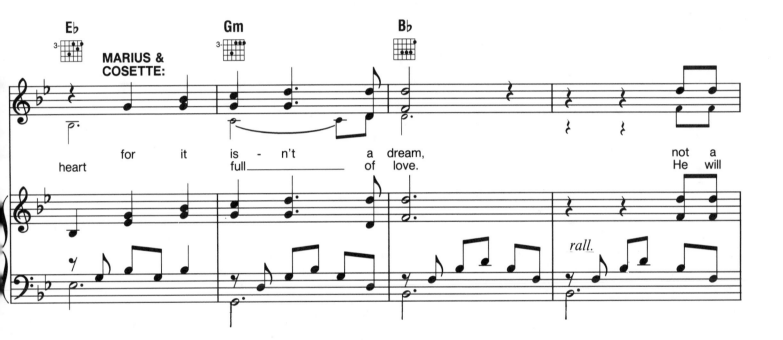

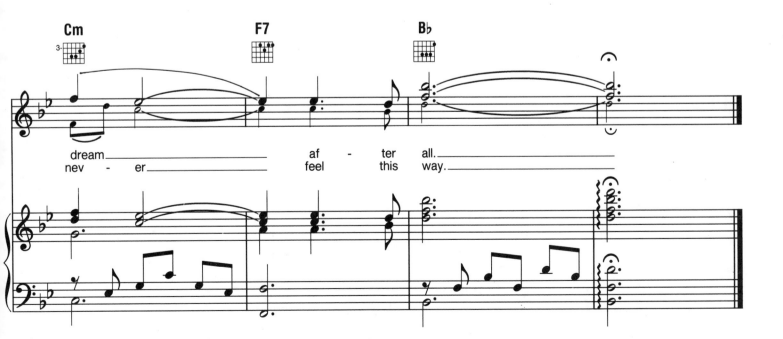

A Little Fall of Rain

Music by CLAUDE-MICHEL SCHÖNBERG
Lyrics by HERBERT KRETZMER
Original Text by ALAIN BOUBLIL and JEAN-MARC NATEL

Drink With Me
(To Days Gone By)

Music by CLAUDE-MICHEL SCHÖNBERG
Lyrics by HERBERT KRETZMER and ALAIN BOUBLIL

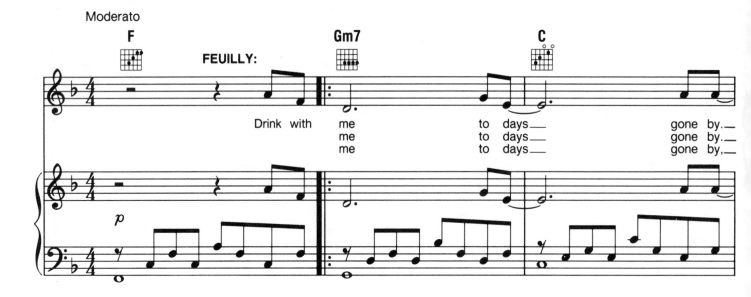

FEUILLY:

Drink with me to days gone by.
me to days gone by.
me to days gone by,

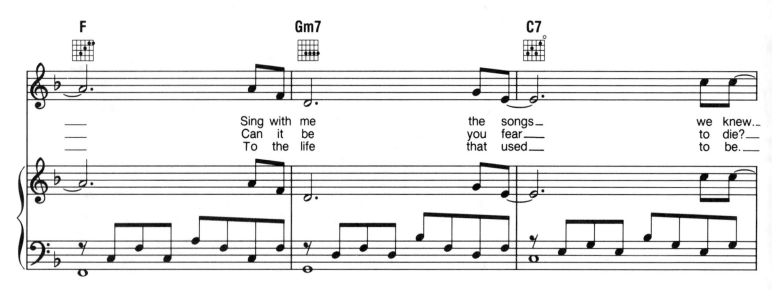

Sing with me the songs we knew..
Can it be you fear to die?
To the life that used to be..

PROUVAIRE: JOLY:

Here's to pret-ty girls who went to our heads. Here's to
Will the world re-mem-ber you when you fall? Could it
At the shrine of friend-ship nev-er say die. Let the

Bring Him Home

Music by CLAUDE-MICHEL SCHÖNBERG
Lyrics by HERBERT KRETZMER and ALAIN BOUBLIL

home.

He's like the son I might have known

più mosso
mf

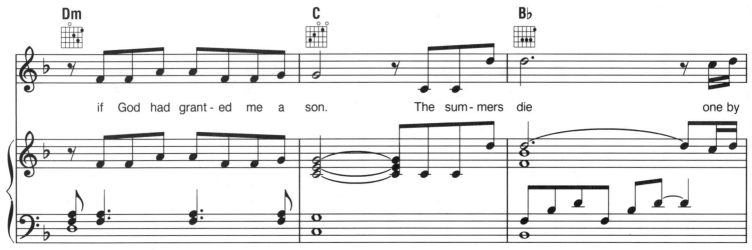

if God had grant-ed me a son. The sum-mers die

one by

one. How soon they fly

on and on. And I am

rit. dim.

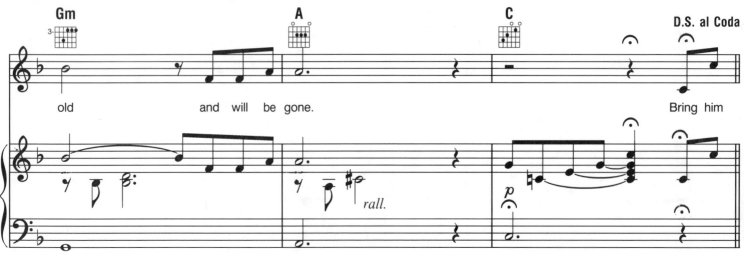

old

and will be gone.

Bring him

D.S. al Coda

rall.

Empty Chairs at Empty Tables

Music by CLAUDE-MICHEL SCHÖNBERG
Lyrics by HERBERT KRETZMER and ALAIN BOUBLIL

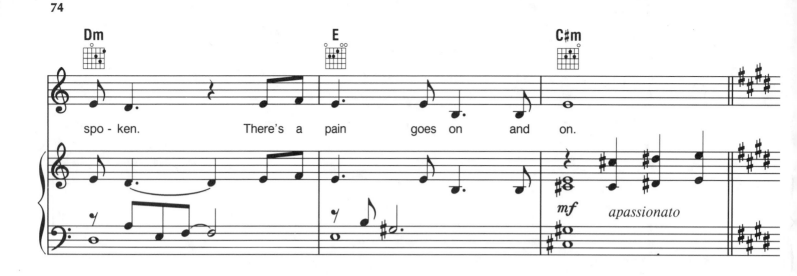

spo - ken. There's a pain goes on and on.

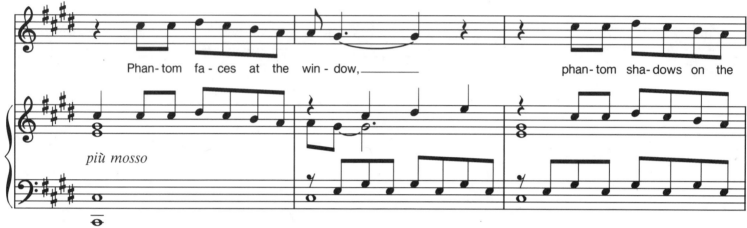

Phan - tom fa - ces at the win - dow,_____ phan - tom sha - dows on the

floor._____ Emp - ty chairs at emp - ty ta - bles where my

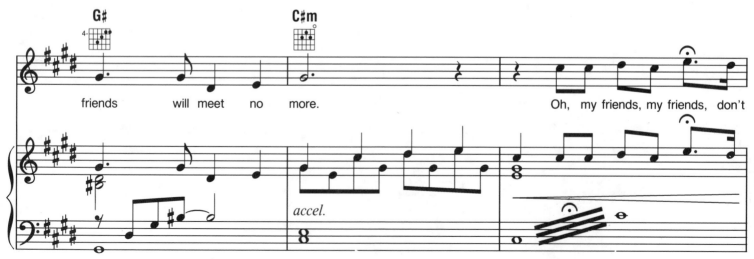

friends will meet no more. Oh, my friends, my friends, don't

On My Own

Music by CLAUDE-MICHEL SCHÖNBERG
Lyrics by ALAIN BOUBLIL, HERBERT KRETZMER, JOHN CAIRD,
TREVOR NUNN and JEAN-MARC NATEL

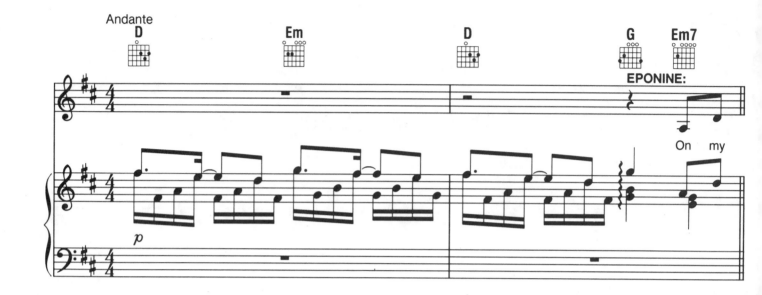

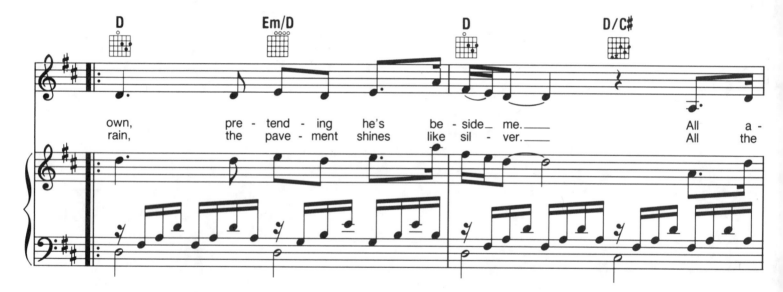

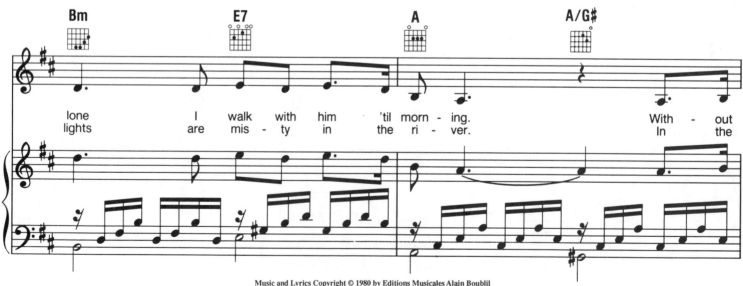